The Simple Simon Drawing Inspiration Book

J. E. Martin

Copyright © 2013 J. E. Martin

All rights reserved.

ISBN-13: 978-1494310745

ISBN-10: 1494310740

Directions:

1. Flip to any page.

2. Read through the word suggestions.

3. Pick out a few words – or even all of them.

4. Use the words as drawing inspiration…

5. …and turn the page into artwork that reminds you of the word suggestions.

6. You can draw, doodle, scribble, or sketch…

7. …anything that enters your imagination.

8. Have fun!

goal artists mysteries fort wisdom puzzle outstanding duty woman train thought crossroads school colossal fictional museum valley pioneer good-humored superb than games race vest little

also daydream privilege independent off food travel
exploding glad disembark comment activities author
maritime facts adventurous enter widespread glowing
subscription model beneath misadventures easy iron

bowling fossil jungle cavern kids dune chuckling find
piracy iridescent buccaneer fascinating spirit our
dazzling from zebras others sincerity survey dearest
unclouded journey shop gorgeous

on threat bird art misery shell striking inspiration break
majestic bus massive daring support inlet list inclusions
elated baskets library see mystic mermaid werewolf plot

long dash everywhere fine make-believe gray word above church explorer insane radiant jolly novels zoo master fun home shale peril escape verity river part danger courage ask perfect monster superlative luminous life jewel selection eager taken under chronicle site arrow additional bad pleasant keen mall general but polished goodness back

harbor lovely brave including archaic appreciate coats
isle themed valor by treaties joyful game signed calling
poor happy-go-lucky berries which group city sea alley
mammals

itinerary ninja vault president greatest them dauntless problem epic year mountain guy beaming whimsical given own you funny during public redeeming strategy shore theater if

conservation closet sunny get microscope gathered noble
great innovative then reliable age done fact hardware
zealous route quest escapade gracious super lively
diamond vampire enchanted

winner planetary quizzes wander honey prepositions
places universe covert verbs check secrecy creativity
caught adventure vivacious splendid giraffes smiling best
comedic shimmering flying extravagant town

those could opportunity hunt path cheetahs hello digging fortress pizza wild cruelly twinkling whale vibrant prize interstellar week archaeology protagonist cleaner ideas feel try ideal cheaters compass first look company government department rivalry settle intergalactic agreement ordinary photograph restaurant suitcase around place animals softened obstacle options browsing hall their leopards happy fairy leader lot time exploratory write emissary yellow critique past man saga amazing lobby no composed investigator ship leave honorable songs vivid police truth profound credit eggs would shellfish spacecraft give how tale primeval undaunted person variety canal only upright risk airplane notorious grand two fantastic globe flight friendship wondrous golden voyage expert expedition secret any includes dinosaur battleship trip commander mother railway harvesting unique point poll map abused enjoyable expect difficult butcher prescription

prints turtles reeds gleaming cattle world roots
convenience living gathering else bravery hunted picking
imagery ready skyscraper jovial seek grocer legend
incredible wonder twin next

conclusions hyenas bold family used poets carefree results
created shelf this forest source now sometimes
circumnavigation oceanic seashore everyday orange
gumshoe right reverie movie charity

nicely amusing embark commute us elaborate excursion thrilling buying office scepter house day post observation heroic she rocket woodland top devotion there gallant elf slow fasten hilarious what with lost bizarre menace insignia published spelling hunting marvelous marine minute osmosis domain footage solve rescue at decked leprechaun he features valiant

station spectacular chase entertaining commit dry
uniform history when courageous grinning regarding
fantasy baker haunted sweet building astute number
darling dragon criteria exploit imagination frost

sunshine store detective spaceship beast different fancy
modern sparkling signal the tell energetic discover faith
poems up utopia they case jumpsuit delighted
magnificent do shores

child cave dogs fishing raft fabulous eye anchor barber creative blue hindrance space wagon local glistening rays apartment caring science pearl castle prehistoric some join necessary because unicorn kind away dream block glittering mission functional book seem park rank evaluating robot princess sand bit island search hope gold me considered knight article amiable citadel desert pursuit sunbeams finding often where curiosity justice sneak we clandestine cliffhanger short story many young resilience gem treasure jubilant obviously

small ocean huge surreptitious curious mild stop cove
trek meeting enjoy beautiful tributary easygoing
ambitious new idea banned creature wouldn't interesting
down coast stone spy

www.ingramcontent.com/pod-product-compliance
Lightning Source LLC
Chambersburg PA
CBHW051829170526
45167CB00005B/2207